THE COLOR LINE

THE PAUL ANTHONY BRICK LECTURES

The Paul Anthony Brick Lectureship was made possible by a generous bequest from Paul Anthony Brick in 1948 to "develop the science of ethics." The lectureship established with that bequest provides for an annual or biennial series of three lectures on ethics to be given at the University of Missouri. The guidelines for the lectures stipulate that they are to address a general audience but should be presented by a scholar with an established reputation. In addition, "The subject matter of the lectureship shall be determined broadly, including ethics not merely in the technical and philosophical sense but also in its relations to literature, society, religion, and other phases of contemporary culture."

THE COLOR LINE

Legacy for the Twenty-First Century

JOHN HOPE FRANKLIN

UNIVERSITY OF MISSOURI PRESS / COLUMBIA AND LONDON

Copyright © 1993 by
The Curators of the University of Missouri
University of Missouri Press, Columbia, Missouri 65201
Printed and bound in the United States of America
All rights reserved
First paperback printing, 1994
5 4 3 2 1   98 97 96 95 94

Library of Congress Cataloging-in-Publication Data

Franklin, John Hope, 1915-
    The color line : legacy for the twenty-first century / John Hope
Franklin.
        p.   cm. — (The Paul Anthony Brick lectures)
    Includes index.
    ISBN 0-8262-0964-5 (pbk.)
    1. United States—Race relations. 2. Racism—United States.
I. Title. II. Series.
E185.615.F69   1993
305.8′00973—dc20   92-38446
                                                                CIP

☺ This paper meets the requirements of the American National
Standard for Permanence of Paper for Printed Library Materials,
Z39.48, 1984.

Designer: Rhonda Miller
Printer and binder: Thomson-Shore, Inc.
Typeface: Trump Mediaeval

To Mary Frances Berry
Courageous Fighter Against the Color Line

CONTENTS

PREFACE

On April 29, 1992, I traveled to the University of Missouri, where I was to begin the Paul Anthony Brick Lectures the following day. My friend and host, Arvarh Strickland, met me at the St. Louis airport and greeted me warmly, and soon we were on our way to Columbia. After exchanging family news, we moved on to discuss the activities of historians, ranging from profound and unique reinterpretations of the field by some of them, to marriages, divorces, deaths, and various other events in their lives. Then, I asked if the jury in the Rodney King trial had reached a verdict. The question gave Arvarh a jolt, for he had heard of the "not guilty" verdict just before my arrival and, in the excitement of our reunion, had failed to mention it. In any case, we were by that time nearing Columbia and could see the news on television.

The verdict had, indeed, been "not guilty," and we were witnessing the first responses to the Simi Valley jury's finding that the four Los Angeles policemen were not guilty of beating and kicking Rodney King. It seemed not to matter that many millions of people around the world had seen the incident, thanks to the recording of it on videotape by an observer. To many this provided incontrovertible evidence of the number and nature of the kicks and beatings that King sustained. Soon, the first fires were flickering in the South Los Angeles area, initiating several days and nights of burning, looting, beating, murder, and other forms of violence.

This was a most tragic response to what the rioters and many others called a gross miscarriage of justice. The events caused many Americans to think again, as they had done on previous occasions that had been triggered by similar events, of the problem of the color line. It appeared that every politician of any consequence, from the president of the United States to other candidates for that office, rushed to the scene. There was the usual wringing of hands, followed by some reference to the persistent problems of the inner city, then a vague promise that more would be done to alleviate conditions there, and finally a return to peace and calm. Concrete proposals to improve economic conditions and the administration of justice did not measure up to the elucidation and analysis of the problem by many would-be statesmen, most of whom provided little more than their presence.

The rationale for moving the trial from Los Angeles to Simi Valley was reminiscent of the plea that counsel for a defendant made to the late Judge Wade H. McCree, Jr., sitting on a lower court before he went to the United States Circuit Court, that the trial of his client should be moved because it would not be possible for a white defendant to get a fair trial before an African American judge. As the Simi Valley trial ended and the decision was rendered, there were those who wondered if Rodney King could get a fair trial in a predominantly white community, with no African Americans on the jury. The verdict confirmed the view of many that he could not.

The riots in Los Angeles continued throughout the time that I was at the University of Missouri to deliver the Brick Lectures; and they provided a dramatic backdrop to the arguments that I advanced in the lectures.

The coincidence of the Brick Lectures and the Los Angeles riots prompted a friend to remark that it was not necessary to burn *all* of Los Angeles to make the point that the color line was still alive and well! I assured her that if I could stop the rioting I would, but I had to concede that events had assisted me in making the points I sought to make. Indeed, it is entirely possible that, even in the aftermath of the Los Angeles riots, I could deliver another set of Brick Lectures on the same subject, using all new materials derived from events that have occurred since April 30, 1992.

The problems of the color line persist as the courts continue to take on cases involving racial discrimination of one kind or another. Numerous examples of racial bias in employment come to light almost daily. The specter of color is apparent even when it goes unmentioned, and it is all too often the unseen force that influences public policy as well as private relationships. There is nothing more remarkable than the ingenuity that the various demarcations of the color line reflect. If only the same creative energy could be used to eradicate the color line; then its days would indeed be numbered.

I was pleased and honored to deliver the Paul Anthony Brick Lectures, and I would like to thank the members of the Brick Lecture Committee who invited me to do so: Lisa Sattenspiel, Roger Cook, Beverly Jarrett, and Bill Bondeson, the committee's chair. The occasion gave me an opportunity once again to reflect on a problem that has not only been with me throughout a lifetime, but one that has been with this country throughout its lifetime. To suggest that the problem of the twenty-first century will be the problem of the color line is not to ignore the changes that have occurred in this as well as in other centuries. It is merely to take notice of the obvious fact that the changes have not been sufficient to eliminate the color line as a problem, arguably the most tragic and persistent social problem in the nation's history.

I have discussed the subject matter of these lectures with colleagues in the institutions where I have taught here and abroad, with business associates, especially in the communications industry, with the students with whom I have been associated for more than a half century, and with friends and neighbors in every community where I have lived. I have learned much from them, and I hope that those lessons are reflected in these lectures as well as in other written and spoken words of mine. I am grateful to them in more ways than I can ever express. My family—my wife, Aurelia, and Whit and Bouna, my sons—have been insightful and critical as we have rehearsed, rehashed, and reviewed the various factors associated with the color line, but most of all they have been supportive and even inspiring. My assistant, Margaret Fitzsimmons, has been a critical and creative editor and overseer. I can never thank them enough; and I could never blame them for whatever shortcomings there are in this work, for those are mine alone.

THE COLOR LINE

I

A NEW BEGINNING
A False Start?

All must share in the productive work of this "new beginning" and all must share in the bounty of a revived economy. With the idealism and fair play which are the core of our system and our strength, we can have a strong and prosperous America, at peace with itself and the world.

From the Inaugural Address by
President Ronald Reagan,
January 20, 1981

Writing at the beginning of this century, the distinguished African American scholar William E. B. Du Bois asserted that the problem of the twentieth century "is the problem of the color line—the relation of the darker to the lighter races of men in Asia and Africa, in America and the islands of the sea."[1] Without any pretense of originality or prescience, with less than a decade left in this century, I venture to state categorically that the problem of the twenty-first century will be the problem of the color line. This conclusion arises from the fact that by any standard of measurement or evaluation the problem has not been solved in the twentieth century, and this becomes a part of the legacy and burden of the next century. Consequently, it follows the pattern that the nineteenth century bequeathed to the twentieth century and that the eighteenth century handed to its successor.

The conclusion of Du Bois was based on his observations of what the country had experienced virtually from the beginning. Eighteenth-century white Americans, in failing to take a stand for human freedom at the time that they were fighting for political independence, gave a clear indication of their values and priorities. They would make the specious claim that they could

1. *The Souls of Black Folk: Essays and Sketches* (New York: The Blue Heron Press, 1953), 13. This edition was published on the fiftieth anniversary of the work's first publication.

not extend freedom to blacks as well as whites because economic and political circumstances would not permit it. In the nineteenth century white Americans, determined to maintain racial segregation, discrimination, and degradation even as chattel slavery ended, would argue that social and economic conditions dictated that sharp distinctions of every conceivable kind be made between white Americans and African Americans.

Observe the status of blacks at the time the nation was born. Even well-to-do property-owning free Negroes, who were required to pay taxes in 1776, were barred from voting. Thus, their own degraded status, whether as slaves or as free persons, made a mockery of the vaunted but inconsistent pleas of the white patriots for justice and equity. In the early days of the republic, free black immigrants were denied eligibility for citizenship; free black men were barred from the United States militia, and in the new capital, Washington, D.C., free blacks were denied the opportunity to vote, hold office, or play any role whatsoever in the political life of the city.

The status of the former slaves in the first two generations following emancipation is a dramatic example of the attempt to make the color line a distinctive and permanent feature of American life. After participating in the political process for less than a decade in the 1860s and 1870s, they were stripped of every vestige of citizenship by one of the most merciless, terror-driven assaults in the annals of modern history. Black men who dared to vote were lynched, and schools that black children dared to attend were burned to the ground, all in the name of the maintenance of high moral and educational standards. These high standards, however, did not disqualify thousands upon thousands of unschooled and unlettered European immigrants from participating in, and even becoming pillars of, a political and social system that was utterly foreign to anything they had experienced or seen.

Du Bois was also disturbed by what he saw occurring in other parts of the world. The partition of Africa and its subsequent brutal exploitation by European powers was something he observed while a graduate student in Europe in the 1890s. A few years before he wrote those prophetic words, he had seen the United States join the family of imperial powers, dealing with Puerto Rico and the Philippines in a manner that reflected its own sense of the superiority of the lighter races of men over the darker races of men, as he would put it.

This, then, is what Du Bois saw as he looked back over two centuries and then peered forward into the ensuing decades. Even as he was predicting that the problem of the twentieth century would be the problem of the color line, new, effective if inane arguments advanced by journalists, politicians, even educators, insisted that the Negro was a beast, a threat to civilization, a drain on the economy, and even a scourge on the body politic. In the wake of these allegations, new patterns of racial segregation and discrimination emerged, along with new forms of racial ostracism and humiliation, and new practices of economic and political degradation. Two world wars did little to expiate the long nightmare of racism in the United States, as racially segregated armies fought to make the world safe for democracy in 1917 and 1918, and as jim crow armies from the United States fought to rid the world of Aryan bigotry from 1941 to 1945.

By the time that Du Bois died in 1963, however, things were looking up; and the most optimistic soothsayers wondered if the color line would confound the twenty-first century as it had nagged its predecessors. Dramatic, even spectacular changes in racial practices and policies occurred following World War II, one of the most significant of which was the remarkable desegregation of the armed forces. Racial segregation in the public schools was outlawed, and in due course racial barriers in public *and* private education at every level began to fall. Congress passed civil rights and voting rights laws in 1957, 1964, and 1965. Meanwhile, more than a score of African Americans sat in the United States House of Representatives, and for a time one was in the United States Senate. They became mayors of major American cities, and they sat in state legislatures from coast to coast.

In the private sector there were numerous outstanding personal achievements. Even as African American newspapers lost ground to white journals that began to "integrate" the news, African American publishers brought out magazines such as *Ebony, Jet, Black Enterprise, Essence,* and *Dollars and Sense* that reached millions of readers. African Americans also began to climb the corporate ladder. For most of them it was a long, arduous, and largely unrewarding journey. A few reached the point where they could see the mountaintop, as it were; nonetheless, if one were to exclude the entertainers and the professional athletes, there were few millionaires among the more affluent members of the African American community.

Perhaps there was cause for optimism as many citizens, white and black, in the public and private sectors, expressed their determination to put behind them the rancor and strife that had characterized race relations for centuries. In 1976 the Democratic candidate for president, Jimmy Carter, ended his campaign with a rally in New York's Madison Square Garden with Martin Luther King, Sr., at his side as all joined in singing "We Shall

Overcome." Following his election, President Carter contributed further to the prevailing optimism by appointing not only the very first African Americans to federal judgeships in the South, but more African Americans to the federal bench, thirty-seven in all, than all previous presidents combined. There were other appointments such as Andrew Young as United States ambassador to the United Nations, and other African Americans to ambassadorial posts in Europe, Africa, and South America. Indeed, during his four years in office Carter made a record number of appointments of both African Americans and women. It appeared that government would lead the way toward racial peace and equity.

There remained, moreover, the legacy of the civil rights movement and the crisis of conscience associated with the Vietnam War. The assassinations of Malcolm X in 1965 and of Martin Luther King, Jr., and Robert Kennedy in 1968 moved many who had remained silent to commit themselves to the fight for racial equality as these three men had done. What kind of barbaric community were Americans living in, some but not too many asked? What was the difference, some asked, between the gangster murderers of the underworld and the blatant assassins of the upper world? It was both disgusting and shameful.

The sobering impact of the Vietnam War drove many Americans to renew their pledge to set things right at home, involving of course the search for racial justice. At the time of the bicentennial of the Declaration of Independence, some Americans vowed to eradicate the persisting influence of the contradictions evident in having fought for independence from Britain while maintaining chattel slavery. The results they achieved cannot be described as spectacular.

Even as Americans made these thoroughgoing and praiseworthy assertions about the need to create a society worthy of the early stated ideals of the nation, there were signs that the real commitment was markedly less than the rhetoric. Perhaps it would be more accurate to say that there were those who believed that the idealism of justice and equality was not nearly as immediately rewarding as the realism of economic and political power.

Already, thanks to the course charted by Kevin Phillips in his *The Emerging Republican Majority*, an increasing number of Americans had begun to give a variety of reasons for their move to the party of Lincoln. "More than a third of a century ago," Phillips observed, "New Deal liberalism rose to power with the coming of age of urban America and its lately arrived immigrant millions. Now the era of the big city in United States politics has come to an end. . . . Old cities like New York, Philadelphia, Detroit, and San Francisco are casting steadily fewer votes, as theirs and other urban populations drain into suburbia. Simultaneously, the Negro socioeconomic revolution and the related bias of the Democratic Party have displaced the Civil War as the underlying divisors of American politics."[2] The new majority would be made up of what Phillips identified as the Catholic working class, white southerners, suburbanites in the Sun Belt, and middle-class Americans sharing a common revulsion against militant minority groups, radical young people, and arrogant intellectuals.

These groups grew in their intensity of feeling against government's providing access for all Americans to the

2. (New Rochelle: Arlington House, 1969), 290. See also the analysis in William Chafe, *The Unfinished Journey: America since World War II* (New York: Oxford University Press, 1986), 383.

nation's resources and opportunities. They also grew in numbers as many Americans saw the increase in the functions of government as an intrusion into people's lives, as an arrogation of authority that rightfully belonged in private hands, and as creating an increased vulnerability to subversive, left-wing influences from the outside as well as the inside. They equated laxity, permissiveness, and defiance of social mores and institutions with nihilism and the breakdown of American society, including greater general freedom for African Americans. Many also equated President Jimmy Carter with ineffectual leadership, lacking the capacity either to solve the energy crisis at home or to do anything about the humiliating hostage situation in Iran. Something had to be done, the sooner the better.

In 1981, the new president of the United States, Ronald Reagan, was already a veteran on the national scene. Not only had he been a movie star of sorts for many years and a two-term governor of California but, in the eyes of some, he had been an almost perennial candidate for the United States presidency, having unsuccessfully sought the Republican nomination for that office in 1968 and 1976. The new Republican majority that swept Reagan into office in 1980 also swept out of office not only his Democratic predecessor but also such durable Democratic liberals as Senators Gaylord Nelson of Wisconsin, Birch Bayh of Indiana, and Frank Church of Idaho.

The agenda of the new administration was set by its supporters of the New Right, who promoted a "new morality" to fight the "master plan to destroy everything that is good and moral here in America," as one advocate put it. There was, moreover, a remarkable growth of "evangelical Christianity," as William Chafe put it, which complemented the new morality and justified vigorous political activity on the part of its adherents. Appealing directly to their followers, the leaders of evangelical Christianity opposed busing, the Equal Rights Amendment, and abortion on demand, while supporting strong family ties, prayer in the schools, and laws against pornography and "deviant" sexual behavior.[3]

It is too much to claim that the president of the United States, by his words and deeds, can unilaterally determine the course of history during his administration and countless subsequent years. It is *not* too much to assert, however, that the president of the United States, through his utterances and the policies he pursues, can greatly influence the national climate in which people live and work as well as their attitudes regarding the direction the social order should take.

As for Ronald Reagan, he made the transition, within a decade or so, from a reformist New Deal Democrat to an activist right-wing Republican. As he did so, he brought with him some of the less attractive baggage that makes a politician feel more comfortable even in his new affiliation. For Reagan, it was telling raunchy, racially offensive jokes and maintaining a disdain for the government's taking a role in promoting equal treatment for blacks. Doubtless he shared the view of his conservative colleagues who believed that blacks lacked the qualities by which they could "make it" in the way that others made it. With no knowledge or understanding of the nature and depth of the fissures in the divisions between white and black, Ronald Reagan was in no

3. *Unfinished Journey*, 460–65.

position to speak for change, to say nothing of setting the course for change.

Reagan was not long in office before he began to contribute to the climate that tolerated racism and, indeed, encouraged policies and measures that denied equal opportunity and equal treatment. Terrel H. Bell, the secretary of the Department of Education, which Reagan had vowed to close when he became president, was appalled by the climate of bigotry he encountered in the Reagan administration. He had heard the president speak out against all forms of discrimination, but either the senior members of the president's staff were not listening or they were certain that the president did not mean to be taken seriously. "I was shocked," Bell said, "to hear their sick humor and racist clichés. When the bill was before the President for his signature or veto to establish a national holiday to honor Martin Luther King, Jr., the President's men referred to the great civil rights leader as 'Martin Lucifer Coon! Ha Ha!', adding that 'We'll soon be able to celebrate Martin Lucifer Coon's birthday.'"[4]

It is well known that nearly 90 percent of African American voters supported President Jimmy Carter in his reelection bid in 1980. It is equally well known that Carter's record of appointing African Americans to high federal office was easily superior to the record of *any* of his predecessors. Reagan's task, once in office, was not so much to use his appointive power to reward the African American faithful, for the number was small. Rather, it should have been to use it to establish better

4. *The Thirteenth Man: A Reagan Cabinet Memoir* (New York: The Free Press, 1988), 104.

lines of communication to the African American community and, in the process, to recruit blacks for what Sidney Blumenthal had aptly called "the permanent campaign" of the New Beginning.[5] Ronald Reagan's appointment of blacks never got beyond the token stage. His choice to head the Department of Housing and Urban Development was Samuel R. Pierce, the African American Wall Street lawyer whose most effective service was to allow his friends to put their hands in the government "cookie jar," as Haynes Johnson put it.[6]

Other appointments of African Americans to the Reagan administration indicate how out of touch with or how indifferent the Reagan people were to the views and needs of African Americans. The president's first choice to head the Equal Employment Opportunity Commission was William Bell, a black consultant from Michigan, who had previously supervised four people and was to move from a relatively moribund office in Detroit to administer a Washington agency that employed more than three thousand people. The absurdity of the appointment led to such an outcry that finally the administration's attempt to secure Senate confirmation was abandoned.

Three months after his inauguration, President Reagan appointed Clarence Thomas as assistant secretary for civil rights in the Department of Education. A year later Thomas was appointed chairman of the Equal Employment Opportunity Commission, a post he would hold until President Bush appointed him in 1989 to the Court of Appeals for the District of Columbia Circuit. Within

5. *The Permanent Campaign: Inside the World of Elite Political Operatives* (Boston: Beacon Press, 1980), 9–10.

6. *Sleepwalking through History: America in the Reagan Years* (New York: Doubleday, 1991), 182.

his year as chairman of EEOC, Thomas made his position clear on affirmative action and other possible sources
of government relief when he said that it was just as
"insane" for blacks to expect relief from the federal
government for years of discrimination "as it is to expect
a mugger to nurse his victim back to health."[7] One can
only wonder if Mr. Thomas, as chairman of the federal
government's EEOC, regarded himself as playing the
role of the mugger! But even before assuming the position of chair of EEOC, Thomas refused in the Department of Education to investigate discrimination complaints to the point that women and minority plaintiffs
asked that Thomas be held in contempt because of his
sloth in pursuing the investigations. Here is the ex-
change between Thomas and the court in the matter of
his refusing to investigate discrimination complaints:

> Q. And aren't you in effect—But you're going ahead and
> violating these time frames [set forth in the requirements
> in *Adams v. Bell* that the civil rights office enforce the
> court's mandate]; isn't that true? You're violating them in
> compliance reviews on all occasions, practically, and
> you're violating them on complaints most of the time, or
> half the time; isn't that true?
> A. That's right.
> Q. So aren't you in effect substituting your judgment as
> to what the policy should be for what the court order
> requires? The court order requires you to comply with this
> 90 day period; isn't that true?
> A. That's right.
> Q. And you have not imposed a deadline [for an Office
> of Civil Rights study concerning lack of compliance with
> the Adams order]; is that correct?

7. "Administration Asks Blacks to Fend for Themselves,"
Washington Post, December 5, 1983, pp. A1, 8.

A. I have not imposed a deadline.

Q. And meanwhile, you are violating a court order rather grievously, aren't you?

A. Yes.[8]

By the time Clarence Thomas had spent the better part of a year in the Office of Civil Rights in the Department of Education, the neglect of initiatives and the indifference to the requirements of the office threatened to dismantle the crucial civil rights effort in education and to reverse the generation of progress toward equal educational opportunity for those young people who most needed the protections to secure an equal chance in education and employment. It is enough to say here that his performance at the Office of Civil Rights was a mere suggestion of what one witnessed at the Office of Equal Employment Opportunity.

In his first year at the EEOC, the length of time to process complaints increased from five months to nine months. The backlog of complaints grew, so that between 1983 and 1987 the backlog doubled from 31,000 to 61,686 complaints, and it continued to rise after 1987. Up to the time that he left the EEOC to join the District of Columbia Court of Appeals, Thomas never laid out a plan for handling the complaints that were, after all, symptomatic of the critical problems of discrimination on the basis of age, sex, race, religion, and so on. It was this stellar performance that caused President Bush to nominate Clarence Thomas as justice of the United States Supreme Court and to declare him to be the best qualified person for that high office.

Since its establishment in 1957 the United States

8. Transcript of Hearing in *Adams v. Bell*, Civil Action 3095-70 (Washington, March 12, 1982), 48, 51.

Commission on Civil Rights had enjoyed remarkable independence from presidential interference, even when it was critical of presidential policies. It had been notably bipartisan, an example of which was the appointment to the commission of a prominent white Republican, Jill Ruckelshaus, by Democratic President Jimmy Carter. In November 1981, his first year in office, President Reagan notified the chairman, Arthur S. Flemming, that he would replace him, the first time in its twenty-four year history that a president had removed a chairman of the Commission on Civil Rights. In Flemming's place, Reagan nominated a conservative black Republican, Clarence Pendleton, who had been executive director of the San Diego Urban League.

A few months later, in an apparent move to revamp the commission completely, the president announced that he would replace Ruckelshaus with the Reverend Sam Hart. A right-wing black evangelical from Philadelphia, Hart was known to be opposed to virtually every item on the civil rights agenda. The furor was so great that Hart's name was withdrawn before it was formally placed before the Senate. Reagan followed this move by sending to the Senate the names of three appointees to replace Mary Frances Berry, Blandina Cárdenas Ramirez, and Murray Saltzman, all known to be critical of the administration's opposition to affirmative action as a remedy for discrimination in employment and education. The nominees, Professor Robert Destro, John Bunzel of the Hoover Institute, and Morris Abrams, were known to have views similar to the president's on matters such as affirmative action in employment.

In his attempt to refashion the commission into a creature that would do his bidding, Reagan created a firestorm in the Senate Judiciary Committee and among a considerable segment of the general public. A compromise provided that the incumbent members would remain, and the president would share his appointive power with the House and the Senate. This infighting and the attempt to undermine the work of the commission resulted in its becoming little more than a debating society. This was a most unfortunate fate for a group that for twenty-five years had done so much to create a favorable climate for racial justice and equality under the law.

As one views the evolution of the Reagan policies in the area of the color line and, indeed, in all areas of public policy, it requires no great intellectual powers to see that the New Beginning of the 1981 administration was committed to nothing less than repealing not only the New Deal of Franklin D. Roosevelt but most of the social innovations since that time.[9]

What the advocates of the New Beginning did not make clear, and what may not have been clear even to the public, was that during the last century, not just the last fifty years, the government had been more actively interventionist than it was willing to admit. Until fifty years ago, however, the intervention was on behalf of a small segment of society that was using government to facilitate its programs to concentrate the major part of the nation's wealth in a relatively few hands. When the United States government subsidized American railroads by granting them millions of dollars and millions of acres of land, it was certainly actively interventionist.

9. For a comprehensive statement on the impact of the Reagan policies on civil rights and the color line, see Drew S. Days, III, "Turning Back the Clock: The Reagan Administration and Civil Rights," *Harvard Civil Rights—Civil Liberties Law Review* 19 (Winter 1984): 309–47.

Government and business formed a partnership that was applauded as a move for the good and glory of all.

What did the New Beginning propose to do about this partnership? President Reagan summed up his economic program in June 1981 when he said, "The ultimate goal of everything we are trying to do is to give this economy back to the American people."[10] This could not be done by presidential fiat, however alluring such a prospect might be. It required programs and plans for the economic benefit of the vast majority of the American people, lest they be cut adrift in a sea of an economic free-for-all where most of them would not have a glimmer of a chance. What of the elderly, the physically handicapped, the orphans, and people on medicaid? What of the president's proverbial "welfare queens," who could not possibly have been as numerous and as profligate as he claimed them to be? If the New Beginning was clear and unequivocal in its plans to reduce benefits for the lower elements of society, it was perhaps more aggressive in promoting policies that would be beneficial to the upper-income groups. The first round of tax cuts was to benefit people with incomes of $50,000 or more, those who owned land that contained oil, and those who were corporate executives or employees of multinational corporations. This was returning the economy to the American people with something more than a flourish!

Put in concrete terms, here is how the economy was returned to the American people: In 1980 there were 574,000 millionaires in the United States. By 1988 there

10. President Reagan's remarks on the program for economic recovery, June 11, 1981. *Public Papers of the Presidents of the United States: Ronald Reagan, 1981* (Washington: Government Printing Office, 1982), 506.

were 1.3 million individual Americans who were millionaires. In 1981 there was a mere handful of billionaires, but by 1988 there were no less than fifty-two American billionaires. Looking at the change in another way, the average income per person of the top 1 percent of Americans increased from $270,053 in 1977 to $404,566 in 1988. Meanwhile, the average income per person of the lowest 10 percent fell from $4,113 in 1977 to $3,504 in 1988.[11] This intensifying inequality, marked by a dramatic redistribution of wealth, was essentially a class phenomenon. With a vast majority of blacks in the lower 40 percent in income, they were especially hard hit by the redistribution of the national income.

No one was more responsible for shaping the New Beginning's policies affecting the color line than William Bradford Reynolds, Reagan's choice for chief of the Civil Rights Division of the Justice Department. As the person charged with enforcing civil rights laws and policies, he brought to trial only two cases involving housing discrimination in his first twenty months in office, compared to nineteen in the last two years of the Carter administration and thirty-two new cases annually during the Republican presidential years of 1969 to 1976. Reynolds refused to use hiring quotas to remedy past job bias, relying on "good faith efforts" on the part of employers to hire more women and blacks. In 1982 he led the fight against an amendment that would have strengthened the Voting Rights Act of 1965. He lost not only the fight but the confidence of every major civil rights organization in the country. Opposed as Reynolds was to mandatory busing and other forms of forced

11. Kevin Phillips, *The Politics of Rich and Poor: Wealth and the American Electorate in the Reagan Aftermath* (New York: Random House, 1990), 8–23.

school desegregation, he and his colleagues opted for voluntary plans and programs such as magnet schools and transfers among urban and suburban school districts to reduce racial segregation.

Perhaps nothing revealed the false start of the so-called New Beginning more than the effort of the Reagan administration to support educational institutions that persisted in adhering to racial discrimination and segregation. Thus, in January 1982, the administration reversed an eleven-year-old policy that denied tax-exempt status to private educational institutions that practiced racial discrimination by reinstating tax exemptions for private schools that discriminated against African Americans and other minorities. That this was a deliberate, calculated policy is attested to by the fact that the decision was made by the secretary of the treasury, approved by the attorney general, and agreed to by the president himself. It was only after a veritable uproar of outrage and disgust from many quarters that the administration offered the feeble excuse that administrative agencies should not exercise powers that the Constitution assigns to Congress. In offering this excuse, the administration overlooked many developments over the years in which all three branches of government have approved the exercise of such powers by the Internal Revenue Service.

By specific legislation Congress had already sanctioned the continuation of existing procedures requiring private schools at least to publish and advertise that they do not practice racial discrimination, as a condition of obtaining tax exemptions. Thus, the institutions that were to be the immediate beneficiaries of the relaxation of the rules, the Goldsboro Christian Schools, which excluded blacks altogether, and the Bob Jones University, which barred interracial dating, were unable to get the tax exemption that the Reagan administration was planning for them. The policy that was now uncovered for what it was moved the *New York Times* to remark that "President Reagan was party to formulating a 'new racist policy'. . . . However obfuscated, however perfumed, that's still tax-exempt hate." Bernard Wolfman said that blacks, like everyone else, "must now pay taxes to a Government that generously rewards racially discriminating schools while it cuts back on financial aid to education generally."[12] Meanwhile, the *Washington Post* called the new policy "outrageous," "a deplorable step backward and one that ignores not only existing laws, but also a series of court decisions."[13]

While the matter was on hold due to the outcry against the proposed reversal of policy, the Bob Jones University sued to have its tax-exempt status restored. That is precisely what the Reagan administration, prompted by W. Bradford Reynolds, the assistant attorney general for civil rights, had intended to do. Obviously, under normal circumstances, it would have been the Department of Justice that would have argued against the university's attempt to interfere with the well-established policy of the Internal Revenue Service. It could not do so in this instance, because the Department of Justice favored what Bob Jones University was seeking. Thus, the anomalous situation developed where the United States Supreme Court had to appoint an outside attorney to present the argument, as a friend of the court, that the Department of Justice refused to present. At least in this case the court-appointed attor-

12. *New York Times*, June 19, 1982, A26, 27.
13. *Washington Post*, June 12, 1982.

ney was several cuts above the average court-appointed attorney, since he was the distinguished African American William T. Coleman, Jr., former secretary of transportation and a senior partner in the Philadelphia law firm of Dilworth, Paxson, Kalish, Levy, and Coleman.

Bob Jones University did not have much of a case, and there was little that the administration could do to help the institution. Meanwhile, the court-appointed attorney, in presenting the case that the federal government should have presented, made short shrift of Bob Jones University's argument that it was entitled to tax-exempt status. Speaking for the court, Chief Justice Warren Burger made it quite clear that the Internal Revenue Service had the authority to withhold tax-exempt status, which it had been doing since 1970. He added that if Congress was dissatisfied with the IRS rulings, it had not expressed it in the eleven years that the IRS had followed the policy of denying tax-exempt status to schools that discriminated against or segregated students on the basis of race. Only Justice William Rehnquist dissented from the court's ruling.[14]

The government, embarrassed and surprised that its proposed new policy evoked such bitter reaction, attempted to make amends by asking Congress to enact legislation that would authorize what the Internal Revenue Service had been doing for eleven years. Most congressional leaders thought new legislation was not necessary, and many felt that this strategy had created a situation for which the administration alone was responsible, and from which it should extricate itself with no assistance from the Congress. It was an object lesson

14. *Bob Jones University v. The United States*, 461 U.S. 574 (1982).

to many citizens, who were revolted by what they saw as an alliance between the administration and the very worst forms of racial bigotry in the land.

When Ronald Reagan called for a New Beginning during the 1980 campaign, it was reminiscent of the sloganeering politics of earlier eras. Whether it was the "New Freedom" of Woodrow Wilson, the "New Deal" of Franklin D. Roosevelt, or the "New Frontier" of John F. Kennedy, the phrases themselves conjured up a new day, perhaps even radically different from what the people had previously experienced. And, in a sense, those visionaries did see a day that was not only different from but better than any they had experienced. Reagan's New Beginning was, in fact, as Thomas Byrne Edsall and Mary D. Edsall have pointed out, a conservative revolution whose governing philosophy was "the insulation of the private sector and the insulation of private citizens from an intrusive government." In Reagan's time this protection shielded them from government whether it was seeking "to regulate industry and commerce" or "to shape the behavior of individual citizens." In articulating a politics of generalized government, the Edsalls continue, "Reagan mastered the excision of the language of race from conservative public discourse." This had the effect of avoiding any head-on confrontation of the question of race and, at the same time, of formulating a policy of governing that targeted policies toward blacks and other minorities without making any reference to race.[15]

It is well to remember that the philosophy of the New Beginning, which called for the insulation of business and property rights from government intrusion, was

15. *Chain Reaction: The Impact of Race, Rights and Taxes on American Politics* (New York: W. W. Norton, 1991), 137–38.

first articulated in 1964 when Ronald Reagan was campaigning for Barry Goldwater. The context then was Goldwater's uncompromising opposition to the Civil Rights Act of that year. And Reagan was able to develop a language that, through setting forth a general rejection of government intrusion, could apply to matters of welfare, busing, and other issues so important to blacks. The language of the proponent of the New Beginning, however, was sufficiently neutral not to be overtly offensive.

Meanwhile, in Texas, where George Bush was attempting to replace Ralph Yarborough in the United States Senate, the civil rights bill became an issue in the senatorial race. Yarborough had voted for the bill in the fall of 1963, when it was in committee, and indicated that he would vote for it when it reached the floor. In March 1964, Bush "warned an audience at the Dallas Country Club of Yarborough's position" and added, "I think most Texans share my opposition to this legislation." He insisted that the bill would make "further inroads into the rights of individuals and the states, and even provide for the ultimate destruction of our trial by jury system."[16] Bush failed in his effort to unseat Senator Yarborough. Likewise, he failed in his effort to predict the impact of the Civil Rights Act of 1964.

It remained to be seen whether, in a country so deeply involved with matters of color, it would be possible for the president of the United States, or indeed any leader, to pursue a policy that claimed to be neutral or color-blind as regards race, and persuade others to accept him as a proponent of justice and equality. While Reagan was elected and reelected by decisive majorities, African

16. Jefferson Morley, "Bush and the Blacks: An Unknown Story," *New York Review of Books* 39 (January 16, 1992), 19–26.

Americans were not impressed, at least those 90 percent of the African American electorate that voted against him in 1980 and 1984. For them the New Beginning was indeed a false start during which time they lost ground in the schoolroom, in the workplace, in social relations, and in the esteem of their fellow human beings.

II

A COLOR-BLIND SOCIETY
Finding the Way?

Our Constitution is color-blind, and neither knows nor tolerates classes among citizens.

From the dissenting opinion of Justice John Marshall Harlan in Plessy v. Ferguson, *1896*

A powerful preoccupying factor in the history of this country since its founding in the seventeenth century has been the matter of color. Color and race have never been far below the level of awareness, even anxiety, on the part of white Americans. The matter of color justified the establishment of African slavery; and then white Americans argued that slavery was not only the natural lot of blacks but the most beneficial state of existence for persons from the "Dark Continent." Indeed, freedom for blacks was not only undesirable but inconceivable. Consequently, every effort should be made to prevent their manumission and even to return to bondage those who were free.[1]

When white Americans were engaged in a life-and-death struggle for their own independence from Britain, they were, at the same time, determined to withhold from blacks those freedoms that whites claimed as their natural right. They were equally determined to keep blacks in a state of perpetual bondage; thus, except for areas where slavery seemed impracticable, such as New England and the Middle Atlantic states, the institution not only grew but flourished—in the Old South and especially in the New Southwest. And as this occurred,

1. For a discussion of the legal aspects of the color line in the colonial period, see A. Leon Higginbotham, Jr., *In the Matter of Color: Race and the American Legal Process* (New York, Oxford University Press, 1978).

slavery became a central feature of southern civilization, a "cornerstone" as some referred to it, an article of faith to which there was a deep and abiding commitment. The Negro race, as William Harper put it in 1837, was inferior to the white race "in mind and character, marked by inferiority of form and features."[2] Harper, who delivered his *Memoir on Slavery* before the South Carolina Society for the Advancement of Learning, was merely one of a long line of men of the South and North who advanced the argument of white supremacy and underscored the importance of the color line in American life.

Among Harper's contemporaries with similar views were Josiah C. Nott, who wrote on the natural history of the Caucasian and Negro races; Thornton Stringfellow, who found in the scriptures ample testimony to support the argument that slavery was a positive good; and Dr. Samuel C. Cartwright, who insisted that the capacities of the Negro adult for learning were equal to those of a white infant. Taking up the cudgel later in the century and carrying it into the twentieth century were Charles Carroll, whose *The Negro a Beast* was a scurrilous attack on blacks as immoral by nature; William P. Calhoun, who stepped up the argument that blacks were inferior; and Robert W. Schufeldt, the title of whose book, *The Negro, a Menace to American Civilization*, dramatically revealed its contents.

By the time that Schufeldt's book appeared in 1907, the arguments regarding the degradation of blacks had gained a new respectability with the emergence of highly esteemed members of the academic community

2. In Drew Gilpin Faust, ed., *The Ideology of Slavery: Proslavery Thought in the Antebellum South, 1830–1860* (Baton Rouge: Louisiana State University Press, 1981), 131.

who couched quite similar views in their treatises on slavery, Reconstruction, and the rise of the New South. With doctoral degrees from some of the nation's most respected universities and with teaching posts at major southern and some northern universities from which African Americans were barred, of course, these so-called scholars catechized their young students regarding the dangers of Negro rule, the importance of racial separation in the regional and national economy, and the tragedy of any move, however slight, in the direction of racial equality. At Columbia University, William Archibald Dunning lectured on the black man's lack of racial pride and his craving for social equality, about which the distinguished historian wrote so passionately in his book on Reconstruction.[3] At Louisiana State University and at Vanderbilt, Walter Lynwood Fleming railed against Negro ignorance, irresponsibility, and criminality, as he had done in his book *Civil War and Reconstruction in Alabama.* At the University of Georgia, E. Merton Coulter lectured on the Negro's inability to control his drinking and his excessive emotionalism in religion, just as he had written as recently as 1947 in his book *The South during Reconstruction.*

One cannot measure with any degree of accuracy the impact of such teaching and writing on regional and national policy or even on etiquette. When one places these later developments beside two centuries of such conduct, one can easily conclude that the impact must have been profound. It is reflected in the veritable mountain of statutes enacted at the close of the last century and in the early years of this century, which went so far as to express in legal terms what constituted

3. *Reconstruction, Political and Economic* (New York: Harper and Brothers, 1907), 213–14.

a black person and a white person. In 1879 Virginia defined a Negro as one possessing one-fourth or more of Negro blood. By 1910, when it was feared that if such persons had the appearance of being white, they would indeed pass for white, the law was amended to include as Negroes all who had one-sixteenth or more Negro blood. To make doubly certain that no black person would fall through possible genetic cracks and be viewed as white, the law was amended—this time in 1930—to read that every person in whom there is "ascertainable any Negro blood shall be deemed and taken to be a colored person."[4]

These definitions of race, which may be regarded as ludicrous by those who were outraged by Germany's Nuremberg laws of 1935, set the tone as well as the racial policies that dominated the period from 1875 to 1910. By that time the racial policies for the twentieth century had been set and needed only the kind of elaboration that is exemplified in the Virginia laws of 1910 and 1930. This was, indeed, a period of wonderment, cast against a background of the new physical, electrical, and biological sciences. But some of the new sciences had their way of making peace with the past. The new Social Darwinism is a case in point, and its accommodation has been described most vividly by Mississippi historian Vernon Lane Wharton:

4. Jno. Garland Pollard, ed., *Pollard's Supplement to the Code of Virginia* (Richmond: Everett Waddey Co., 1910), sect. 19, p. 16; *The Code of Virginia as Amended to Adjournment of General Assembly 1930* (Charlottesville: The Mitchie Co., 1930), sect. 62, p. 26. See also *The Negro in Virginia, Compiled by Workers of the Writers Program of the Works Project Administration in the State of Virginia* (New York: Hastings House, 1940), 237ff.

It produced the laissez-faire sociology of William G. Sumner and the racist political science of John W. Burgess, while it welcomed the importation of the harsh economic doctrines of David Ricardo and Alfred Marshall. It was the time when presidents and professors of great universities joined newspaper editors and Supreme Court justices in scientific condemnation of any effort to relieve the lot of those whose poverty and wretchedness were adequate proof of inferiority; and when the recorded lynchings of almost 2,000 Negroes in twenty years could be shrugged off, defended as necessary, or applauded.[5]

This is what W. E. B. Du Bois was observing when he said that the problem of the twentieth century would be the problem of the color line. Even as he uttered words that were remarkably wise and prescient, it is difficult to believe that Du Bois fully appreciated the ramifications of what was occurring. He could see, of course, the growing disparity between educational opportunities for black children and those for white children. He was aware of the mounting wall of segregation that kept the races from having any civilized contact or discourse. He observed the discrimination in the workplace that gave no consideration to the comparative qualifications of black and white applicants for a given job. But it would take the wisdom of the ages to see the profound impact that several centuries of preoccupation with undervaluing an entire race of people could have on the moral fiber of a nation, and on the national psyche.

5. "Reconstruction," in Arthur S. Link and Rembert W. Patrick, eds., *Writing Southern History: Essays in Historiography in Honor of Fletcher M. Green* (Baton Rouge: Louisiana State University Press, 1965), 298.

By the middle of the twentieth century, the color line was as well defined and as firmly entrenched as any institution in the land. After all, it was older than most institutions, including the federal government itself. More important, it informed the content and shaped the lives of those institutions and the people who lived under them. Imagine, if you can, a country where blacks and whites were transported in separate elevators, where telephone booths were designated by race, and where the school textbooks were stored during the summer months in warehouses based on the race of those who had used them the previous term. If only we could be as sensitive to the problem of AIDS in 1992 as we were to the risk, whatever it was, to white children who in 1902 used books that had previously been handled by African American children!

Thus have we lived in this century in the theater of the absurd. Black men and women pleaded for an opportunity to serve their country during World War I. Begrudgingly, the United States military admitted them, but would not have them in its own armed forces. Instead, they were shunted into the French army, where they performed with great valor. Hundreds of them received France's highest military honor, the Croix de Guerre, but, in the judgment of the United States, *not one* of them had been brave enough or intrepid enough to receive their own country's highest recognition for valor, the Medal of Honor. The same was true of World War II seaman Doris Miller. Without any previous experience under fire, he manned a machine gun during the Japanese attack on Pearl Harbor and shot down four enemy planes. Similar incidents of sacrifice and valor were numerous, but in the face of such heroism it is interesting to recall that a 1990 National Opinion Research Report recorded that more than 50 percent of American whites believed African Americans were less patriotic than white Americans![6]

Perhaps the whites in that survey were really trying to understand what might go through an African American's mind when the national anthem refers to "the land of the free" or the Pledge of Allegiance speaks of "liberty and justice for all" or the Declaration of Independence proclaims that all human beings are "created equal." If one is an African American, these high-sounding phrases do not, cannot, mean what they mean to a white American. "It is not that you are 'disloyal,'" Andrew Hacker remarks. "Rather, you feel no compelling commitment to a republic that has always rebuffed you and your people."[7]

As he neared the middle of the century, W. E. B. Du Bois saw no reason to change his prediction that the problem of the twentieth century would be the problem of the color line. Indeed, what he saw merely reaffirmed what he had said. He had worked hard to make his prediction inaccurate. Writing, speaking, marching, fighting against injustice and inequality from the beginning of his long and distinguished career, he began to wonder if it had all been in vain. He said that the veil of color

drops as drops of night on southern seas—vast, sudden, unanswering. There is Hate behind it, and Cruelty and Tears. As one peers through its intricate, unfathomable pattern of ancient, old, old design, one sees blood and guilt and misunderstanding. And yet it hangs there, this Veil,

6. Tom W. Smith, *Ethnic Images*, GSS Topical Report no. 19 (Chicago: NORC, December 1990).

7. *Two Nations: Black and White, Separate, Hostile, Unequal* (New York: Charles Scribner's Sons, 1992), 47.

between then and now, between Pale and Colored and Black and White—between you and me. Surely, it is but a thought-thing, tenuous, intangible; yet just as surely is it true and terrible and not in our little day may you and I lift it.[8]

Tragically, Du Bois sank deeper in his pessimism and depression. Disillusioned because the problem was as alive and as intractable in his ninetieth year as it had been sixty years earlier, he gave up on it, became an expatriate, and spent his remaining years in Ghana. Du Bois left not only a rich legacy of doing battle to destroy the color line but the legacy of the problem that he could not solve and that, to him, by the early 1960s seemed insoluble.

In the final decade of the life of Du Bois and in the decades that followed, many Americans insisted that we were at long last creating a society that was color-blind. The courts did their part in such landmark decisions as *Brown v. The Board of Education*, outlawing segregation in the public schools; another decision asserting that affirmative action was an appropriate way to address discriminatory patterns and practices; and yet another case where the court said that the Civil Rights Act of 1866 outlawed private acts of discrimination, even in a children's day-care center that sought to deny admission to a child because he was an African American.[9]

The Congress at times took the initiative by enacting strong civil rights acts in 1957 and 1964, by passing the Voting Rights Act in 1965, and by setting up institutions

8. *The Autobiography of W. E. B. Du Bois: A Soliloquy on Viewing My Life in the Last Decades of Its First Century* (New York: International Publishers, 1968), 411.

9. *Brown v. Board of Education*, 349 U.S. 294 (1954); *Griggs v. Duke Power Company*, 401 U.S. 424 (1971); and *Runyon v. McCrary*, 427 U.S. 160 (1976).

such as the Commission on Civil Rights, the Equal Employment Opportunity Commission, and a Community Relations Service to assist individuals and communities in coping with problems involving race and gender. These acts and agencies enjoyed varying degrees of success. Their importance lay as much in the climate they created by indicating the federal government's interest in such matters as in their actual achievements.

To round out the picture, the executive branch fell in line and, for the moment, seemed not to be a hindrance in launching a color-blind society. President Dwight D. Eisenhower, who, as a World War II general, had opposed the desegregation of the military, accepted with grace his role in implementing the Civil Rights Act of 1957 and with something less than grace the Supreme Court decision in *Brown v. The Board of Education*. He declined to express "approbation or approval" of the decision and said that he did not believe "that you can change the hearts of men with laws or decisions." The Supreme Court has spoken, he said, "and I am sworn to uphold the Constitutional process in this country. I will obey."[10] Nevertheless, he sent federal troops into Little Rock, Arkansas, in 1957 to break the governor's defiance of the order to admit African American students to the all-white high school.

Richard M. Nixon seemed more preoccupied with establishing a Republican majority than with racial peace. Thus, in 1971 he warned federal officials to stop pressing for the desegregation of southern schools through "forced busing," one of the many race-coded phrases designed to bring segregationists into the Republican

10. *Public Papers of the Presidents of the United States: Dwight D. Eisenhower, 1954* (Washington: Government Printing Office, 1955), 491; see also 1066.

fold. "I am against busing as that term is commonly used in school desegregation cases," Nixon remarked. "While the executive branch will continue to enforce the orders of the Court . . . I have instructed the Attorney General and the Secretary of Health, Education, and Welfare that they are to work with individual school districts to hold busing to the minimum required by law."[11]

It was not difficult for Nixon's immediate successors to out-distance him in the quest for racial equality. Gerald Ford was remarkably nonpartisan and racially color-blind in the positions he took and the appointments he made. If Nixon consciously cultivated the racists who worked for a Republican majority, Ford's effort to restore faith and integrity in the presidency after Nixon's disgrace and resignation brought a modicum of stability to the volatile climate of race relations.

As we have already seen, Jimmy Carter set records in a variety of areas where African Americans were concerned. He appointed African Americans to important positions that had been the exclusive domain of whites. Thus Andrew Young, a former member of Congress from Georgia, became the United States ambassador to the United Nations. President Carter sought in a variety of ways to reinvigorate federal policy in the enforcement of the federal laws looking toward racial justice that had been passed before he took office. In his concern with affairs in Africa, where he traveled extensively, Carter indicated his appreciation of the international dimensions of the problem of race. What was quite clear in his administrative policies is that African Americans were regarded as a respected and worthy constituency and as being as deserving as all other Americans.

11. *Public Papers of the Presidents of the United States: Richard Nixon, 1971* (Washington: Government Printing Office, 1972), 848.

One is tempted to wonder what would have happened, what might have happened, had not the Republican party sensed that it could capitalize on the prevailing racist climate by appealing to and welcoming into its folds the opponents of racial equality and justice. Those opponents, many of them lodged in the Democratic party since Reconstruction, began to feel uncomfortable there as far back as 1948 when President Truman began to desegregate the armed forces and speak out against segregation in general. When he went along with his party's 1948 platform calling for racial justice and equality, some old-line Democrats "took a walk," created a States Rights party, and never returned to the party of their forebears. South Carolina's Strom Thurmond was the presidential candidate of the new party. Unable to defeat Truman by splitting the Democratic party, many of them, including Thurmond, found a permanent home in the Republican party, where they were welcomed with open arms.

In succeeding years, more disaffected Democrats moved into the Republican party. The attractions were several: a strong anti-communist stand on foreign policy when the Democrats, among whom were liberals and radicals, seemed soft on "reds"; a generally conservative stance that favored less government involvement in the economy when the Democrats were dreaming of a Great Society that placed the government on center stage; and a racial policy that stressed law and order and restraint on fast-paced integrationists when African Americans seemed to be gaining in influence in the high councils of the Democratic party.

The new realignments were not all that comfortable for either political group. Having in their midst a growing number of new members whose motive was to find a haven for their conservative racial views, even the Republicans who did not share the views of the Strom Thurmonds were not inclined to make their new colleagues feel unwelcome. In any case, the party's racial politics precluded any crusade or, indeed, any support for public intervention to improve the status of African Americans. The Democratic party, on the other hand, was somewhat embarrassed by the increasing number of its African American members and supporters, and by its increasing identification with "causes" that some Americans described as extreme and, in any case, beyond the purview of governmental involvement.

It was at this juncture—when public policy generally, and the work of the three branches of government in particular, had created a climate so favorable to racial justice and equality—that many white Americans began to talk about our society as being color-blind. And if we had not arrived at that happy state, conditions were in place that would be especially helpful in rapidly advancing us to that state. Indeed, some argued, the surest way to becoming a color-blind society was to assume that we were already in one.

Unfortunately, the litigation, legislation, and executive implementation, however effective some of it was, did not wipe away three centuries of slavery, degradation, segregation, and discrimination. Nothing that had happened in the past forty or fifty years had created a society in which the factor of color was not a major consideration in virtually everything Americans thought, said, or did. The decision in *Brown* waved no magic wand, although many of its opponents as well as its supporters believed it to be the supreme law of the land which must be obeyed. The Voting Rights Act, with all the resources of the federal government at its disposal to enforce it, did not move African Americans closer to wielding political power commensurate with their numbers, or even eliminate racial politics as a major factor in any election. What these public policies and actions did do, among other things, was to persuade untold numbers of Americans that it was somehow inappropriate for them to crusade for racial equality that presumably had been achieved in the newly recognized color-blind society.

This attitude led logically to the view that neither the individual nor the state had any responsibility in seeing to it that new Supreme Court decisions, new legislation, or new executive orders required the support of *all* Americans in moving toward a color-blind society in which African Americans enjoyed the same protection as other Americans. But too many Americans equated equal protection with equal jeopardy. Thus, they reasoned, now that African Americans enjoyed *equal* protection of the laws, they needed no *special* protection of the laws. Those who had counseled the social engineers not to go too fast seemed willing overnight to embrace the concept of a color-blind society that offered neither favors nor even protection based on color. The consequences of such a position were dire indeed, for the view was vigorously advanced that it was even improper to offer protection to those entering a period of transition leading to genuine equality.

The reasoning behind the opposition to any specific programs or machinery to facilitate equal employment opportunities or hiring goals, or even measures such as busing to achieve desegregated schools, was that such measures were unnecessary. No implementation was required, many insisted. They went one step further. Not only was implementation unnecessary, it was undesirable because it conferred special favors on one group, thus discriminating against other groups. And if it was undesirable it should be opposed. Such a line of reasoning could and did lead to the argument that, in a color-blind society, it was counterproductive to take steps to assist persons in their effort to achieve equality or to protect them from mistreatment or exploitation by persons of another color. The only thing wrong with this argument is that it is based on an assumption that flies in the face of the facts. A color-blind society does not exist in the United States and never has existed.

In his opinion in *Plessy v. Ferguson*, which was decided in 1896, Supreme Court Justice John Marshall Harlan, born and raised in Kentucky, said, "Our Constitution is color-blind, and neither knows nor tolerates classes among citizens."[12] This view of Justice Harlan was one devoutly to be wished. At least three factors qualified the views he expressed. One was that his was a dissenting opinion in which he denounced the court for upholding the separate but equal provisions of the Louisiana segregation statute. The prevailing view of the majority of the court was that the Constitution was *not* color-blind. It could even see color where the average person could not. Plessy, one-eighth Negro, had no recognizable features of a man of color and was arrested when riding in a coach reserved for white people only because the conductor knew who he was.

Second, Justice Harlan perhaps borrowed his rhetorical flourish from Albion Tourgee, who was the attorney for Plessy and who had asserted in his brief that "Justice is pictured blind and her daughter, the Law, ought at least to be color-blind."[13] Tourgee's experiences in North

12. 163 U.S. 537 (1896).
13. The Plessy brief, written by Tourgee, is in Albert P. Blaustein and Robert L. Zangrando, *Civil Rights and the American Negro: A Documentary History* (New York: Trident Press, 1968), 298–304.

Carolina during Reconstruction had taught him that American society was not color-blind, but that did not deter him from believing that the law *should* be if justice was to be evenhanded.[14]

Third, Justice Harlan was expressing the same ideal he had expressed thirteen years earlier when he was the lone dissenter in the civil rights cases, when the Supreme Court said that Congress had no authority under the Civil Rights Act of 1875 to prevent states from segregating African Americans and discriminating against them.[15] He knew that society in the United States in 1896 was not color-blind, but he wanted his colleagues to understand that the Constitution was a living, evolving instrument that *could* be color-blind if the people who lived under it came to believe sincerely that there should be no discrimination based on color, race, or previous condition of servitude.

Neither the courts nor the Congress nor the president can declare by fiat, resolution, or executive order that the United States is a color-blind society. They can only facilitate a movement in that direction by discharging their duties in a way that reflects their commitment to such a goal. From that point on, it is the people of all colors who must work in every way possible to attain that goal. Those who insist that we should conduct ourselves as if such a utopian state already existed have no interest in achieving it and, indeed, would be horrified if we even approached it.

It is fascinating to listen to the arguments of those who claim that our laws and policies should never

14. For an account of Tourgee's experiences in North Carolina see his novel *A Fool's Errand by One of the Fools.* A convenient rendition was edited by John Hope Franklin in the John Harvard Library (Cambridge: Belknap Press of Harvard University Press, 1961).

15. 109 U.S. 3 (1883).

contradict the concept of a color-blind society. We should not even take cognizance of such things as racial distinctions. Thus, legislation, proclamations, executive orders, and policy directives that seek to correct societal defects based on color should be repealed, rescinded, and revoked. They go so far as to argue that the public, in adhering to racial neutrality, should ignore, even oppose, private and public programs that are color-conscious. Thus, in 1984, the president of the United States visited Charlotte, North Carolina, and denounced school busing as especially out of place in a fast-moving, energetic, twentieth-century urban community that should take no notice of color. The Democrats, the president said, "favor busing that takes innocent children out of the neighborhood school and makes them pawns in the school experiment that nobody wants. We've found out it failed."

Charlotte had one of the most exemplary busing programs in the country. Because the community was keenly aware of its own needs in the area of color and race and did not claim to be color-blind, it had worked out, among other things, a highly successful busing program that effectively desegregated the Charlotte public schools. This followed the unanimous Supreme Court decision of 1971 that sanctioned the use of quotas, gerrymandering, and busing to achieve desegregation.[16]

Small wonder that the proud citizens of Charlotte took exception to the president's uninformed strictures. Jay Robinson, the superintendent of schools, was not pleased. He declared that the citizens of Charlotte had developed "a tremendous amount of pride" in the success of their busing program. One county commissioner

16. *Swann v. Charlotte-Mecklenburg Board of Education,* 402 U.S. 1 (1971).

dismissed Reagan's remarks as "bull." The president of the State Board of Education, C. D. Spangler, wondered why the president should attempt to undermine a unanimous ruling by the United States Supreme Court. The *Charlotte Observer* spoke for many when it carried an editorial under the forthright caption, "You are wrong, Mr. President." The editor asked, "Where did he get his information that busing in Charlotte had failed. From Jesse Helms? If you had talked to some of the good Republicans here you would have found that many of them are very proud of their public schools and would fight anyone—even you—who tried to destroy what this community had accomplished."[17]

After a Supreme Court decision in March 1992, it is possible that President Reagan will now regard himself as vindicated. In a case arising in DeKalb County, Georgia, where authorities declared that they had done all that they could do to desegregate the schools, the court, speaking through Justice Anthony Kennedy, assented to their claim. It said that the federal district court need not retain active control over every aspect of school administration, including busing, "until a school district has demonstrated unitary status in all facets of the system." In other words, a school district is not necessarily in violation of the consent decree under which the district court supervises its desegregation program, as long as the program has resulted in the elimination of de jure segregation in some if not all facets of the system.[18] At least the former president would be pleased that his appointees to the Supreme Court were in agreement that the government should get off the backs of the people!

17. *Charlotte Observer,* October 9, 1984.
18. *Freeman v. Pitts,* no. 89-1290, March 31, 1992.

Perhaps one of the worst things about the claim that we live in a color-blind society is that when the assertion comes from responsible officials who know better, it provides cover for those who seek to exploit the factor of race. President Reagan, his attorney general, and the assistant attorney general for civil rights shared that view. Legal remedies that sought to promote civil rights were, therefore, out of place because they automatically raised the specter of a problem of color that did not, in their view, exist. Thus, in 1982 they opposed the amendments to the Voting Rights Act that outlawed intentional discrimination as well as practices that resulted in discrimination. They opposed, without exception, affirmative action policies looking toward the effective elimination of discrimination against minorities and women and urged the states to do the same. They virtually destroyed, presumably as unnecessary in a color-blind society, the United States Commission on Civil Rights that was established in 1957 to monitor discrimination based on race.

Various ones among these highly placed officials attacked, by name, justices of the United States Supreme Court whose opinions were abhorrent to them. Attorney General Edwin Meese went so far as to reject the historic notion, at least as old as *Marbury v. Madison* in 1803, that the Supreme Court had the power of judicial review and that its decisions were, therefore, *not* the supreme law of the land. In a word, the government of the United States, through its chief law enforcement officials, declared war on American law, on judicial decisions, and on public policies they happened to dislike. This moved Stanford law professor Paul Brest, in a piece called "Meese, the Lawman, Calls for Anarchy," to declare, "Our tradition of according the judicial branch the last word on constitutional questions reflects our dedication to the rule of law. One may, therefore, wonder why at this of all times, an Attorney General committed to 'law and order' would propose a policy so likely to encourage disrespect for the courts."[19]

The very worst consequence of the claim that we live in a color-blind society and can ignore the law if we disagree with it is that already Americans have responded to this cordial invitation to anarchy. The Ku Klux Klan has taken heart and embarked on an effort to resurrect a patently racist, terrorist organization. Only when some of its leaders sought the cloak of respectability by running for public office as members of the Republican party did some party members begin to express disapproval. In an atmosphere of tolerance of racial bigotry parading under the banner of racial neutrality, white students have been encouraged to intimidate, terrorize, and make life miserable for African American students at many of our institutions of higher learning.

The task of overcoming the active encouragement of anarchy and terror in a country where the concept of a color-blind society is as specious as the concept of perpetual motion is stupendous. It is dismaying to observe that there has been no significant, even discernible change in the drift or the course of our government in such matters in recent years. In 1990 President Bush made two trips to North Carolina to campaign for the reelection of the senior senator from that state, Jesse Helms. In doing so, he spoke out against the proposed civil rights restoration bill as a "quotas bill," thus handing Helms his most effective argument. By creating

19. *New York Times*, November 2, 1986.

the impression that affirmative action would take jobs away from whites and give them to blacks, Bush raised both fear and hate that translated into votes and made Helms the winner in November 1990.

A color-blind society eludes us. For one reason, we have not sought diligently and conscientiously to pursue it. It is one thing to mouth the words, but it is quite another to perform the deeds. For another reason, I do not believe that we as a nation appreciate what constitutes a color-blind society. To some of us it means the homogenization of our individual cultures to the point that they are no longer recognizable or identifiable. To others it means subordinating a group's aspirations to the interests of the nation as a whole. Du Bois discovered in 1917 that this could lead to nowhere as he summoned all African Americans to "close ranks" in support of the war effort. When the war was over, in which nearly a half-million African Americans had served their country, they were beaten back into the "place" designated for them in a series of race riots, the bloodiest the nation had ever seen.

A final reason a color-blind society eludes us is that we do not wish to find it. A balkanized racial differentiation has been remarkably profitable and even satisfying to many people. In a color-blind society, how would one find a group so easily and automatically exploitable? In a color-blind society, how could one racial group be squared off against another, as in a cockfight, with the sponsors, not the winner, taking all? In a color-blind society, how could racial and social groups deficient in virtually every conceivable way rest comfortably without the satisfaction of knowing that those of darker hue were less fortunate and more degraded than they?

To find the way out of this morass, these dilemmas, is

the great challenge of this decade. It is also our final opportunity to prevent the color line from being a most important legacy for the twenty-first century.

III

A NEW CENTURY
A New Nation?

Let America be America again.
Let it be the dream it used to be.
Let it be the pioneer on the plain
Seeking a home where he himself is free.

Langston Hughes

The years following World War II were turbulent in many ways. The world had entered the nuclear age, fraught with so many dangers, especially as the superpowers seemed destined and determined to make the cold war as frightening as the fighting war had been. Around the world the darker peoples were rising up and throwing off the controls that the imperial powers had imposed for many decades. In Asia and Africa they were declaring their independence; in Latin America they were restive and experimenting with new social and economic systems. Ethnic and religious rivalries were keen as Christians, Muslims, and Jews vied for favors in terms of territory, power, and commitment.

The United States was, in many ways, a microcosm of what was transpiring elsewhere. If there was an uneasy peace abroad, violence in the United States was increasing. African Americans, unhappy with their own predicament, took their cue from the new African nations and began to refer to themselves as a colonial people. For a time, even the religious rivalries were replicated here as the Nation of Islam sought to solve for blacks the problems about which no one else seemed to be sufficiently serious, or certainly not sufficiently committed, to address. What was most distressing was that whatever the changes, whatever the dramatic achievements in the lives of individual African Americans, those somehow were not credited to the group in general.

Perhaps they should not have been, but they should not have had the opposite effect either. All too often, the reaction was that if one made remarkable progress, the achiever was not an exceptional American but an exceptional African American. He or she had demonstrated extraordinary talent, acumen, or courage in beating overwhelming odds—obviously placed in his or her way not by society or those who called attention to them, but by some little gremlin. Underneath the fulsome praise was more than a slight suggestion that he or she was the exception that proved the rule.

Meanwhile, little could be said of the mass of African Americans, huddled in the poorest possible sections of crowded cities or experiencing the indescribable desolation of rural poverty, except that they were both powerless and virtually helpless. The violence that was all too characteristic of much of the inner city was hurled, as if by centrifugal force, into direct conflict with whites, thus spawning the riots and general racial disorders of the 1960s that spread from one community to another. If any American can remember or has read of the riots in the summer of 1967 in cities such as Newark, Detroit, and more than a score of others, that person knows that many American communities began to unravel. The tragedy lay not only in the injuries and death and destruction of property, but in the breakdown of discourse and virtually all lines of communication between two groups of people who had inhabited the same area since the early seventeenth century. Now they were barely speaking to each other, if at all. And all they seemed able to do was to lick their wounds and express their bitterness and discontent.

Sensing the potential volatility of the situation, President Lyndon B. Johnson appointed a National Advisory

Commission on Civil Disorders. After spending seven months looking at the problem over much of the United States, the commission reached one basic conclusion that was as dramatic in impact as it was unpretentious in the way it was stated. "Our nation," the report declared, "is moving toward two societies, one black, one white—separate and unequal."[1] After pointing out that the deepening racial division that it described was not inevitable, it made a series of hard-hitting recommendations. To shore up the economy, especially among the disadvantaged, the commission called for the creation of 2 million new jobs in the next three years. To improve the educational system, the commission called for accelerated integration "as a priority education strategy" as well as for a dramatic improvement in the quality of education. There were other recommendations such as reforming the welfare system, improving housing, expanding the Model Cities Program, and eliminating discrimination in the public and private sectors.

The commission doubtless felt good about what it had done. One witness appearing before the commission, Dr. Kenneth B. Clark, made some observations that must have been sobering in their effect, however. Referring to the commission's work and to the reports of similar commissions going back to World War I, Clark said, in part,

> I read that report . . . of the 1919 riot in Chicago, and it is as if I were reading the report of the investigating committee on the Harlem riot of '35, the report of the investigating

1. *Report of the National Advisory Commission on Civil Disorders* (New York: Bantam Books, 1968), 1.

committee on the Harlem riot of '43, the report of the Cone Commission on the Watts riot.

I must again in all candor say to you members of this commission—it is a kind of Alice in Wonderland—with the same moving picture re-shown over and over again, the same analysis, the same recommendations, the same inaction.[2]

Even if he did not have Kenneth Clark's critical view in mind, Andrew Hacker, in choosing the title of his study on the problem of race in America, surely did not think that things had improved markedly by 1992.[3] Hacker was quite mindful of the 1968 report and, indeed, was thinking of it when he decided to give his book a title that clearly indicated that there had been little change since the commission's report in 1968. Obviously he thought that the 1968 report was too sanguine and did not sufficiently take into account the long, tragic history of race relations in the United States. In any case, Hacker's work is a corrective to the 1968 report on two counts. First, he recognized how thoroughly corrosive the entire relationship of blacks and whites had been over the years, bringing in its wake the inequality and hostility that extended back at least three centuries and longer, if the Elizabethan attitudes are taken into account.[4] This led to Hacker's second observation, namely, that there can be no "quick fix" for a situation hoary with age and interlayered with so many complex sociological, anthropological, and historical problems that it cannot be addressed in a casual or even a merely serious

2. Ibid., 483.
3. *Two Nations: Black and White, Separate, Hostile, Unequal.*
4. Winthrop D. Jordan, *White over Black: American Attitudes Toward the Negro, 1550–1812* (Chapel Hill: University of North Carolina Press, 1968).

manner. The approach must be informed by a thorough understanding of the very complex problems that produced the situation in the first place. We would be immensely rewarded if we could merely delineate the situation as it exists today, and try to see how we arrived at this juncture. It will require wiser heads to lay out the solution, although one should not minimize the importance of recognizing the nature and the parameters of the problem as a significant step to its resolution.

The color line has been a persistent factor in the history of this country and especially in the African American's effort to become an integral part of American society. For most of our history the schools have been segregated, and, since the power to allocate resources has invariably been in the hands of whites, that has inevitably meant placing African Americans at an almost hopeless disadvantage. All of us, black and white, should be aware of the nature of the color line in American education. For a black child, it has meant the expenditure of one-half, one-fourth, or less for his or her education than for the education of a white child. Sixty years ago in my home state of Oklahoma an African American had the unattractive option, after graduating from an inferior high school, of going to a miserably poor all-black college or leaving the state to pursue higher education at his or her own expense. And one could not return at all to the state to pursue graduate or professional studies. Blacks were simply barred from professional and graduate schools in the state. At that time an African American could not even live in the town of Norman, Oklahoma, where the university was located. Meanwhile, the state of Missouri and many other states were scarcely better.

Imagine, if you can, the kind of education about the

world, about the peoples of Africa, or about African Americans that white students received in the 1930s in such racially antiseptic, lily-white institutions as the University of Oklahoma or the University of Missouri or Princeton or Notre Dame. And yet it is the graduates of such institutions during that period who have had so much to say about the public policies of their communities regarding race and all other matters from that day to this.

This is not to suggest that such institutions were the training ground for the neo-Nazis, the Ku Klux Klan, or the skinheads of the 1990s, although some of these miscreants were doubtless enrolled in the very classes from which African Americans were excluded. It is to suggest that those who should have known better, and who could have created a climate that would have been inhospitable to such dangerous groups, were not prepared to "take them on." They were insensitized to the deadly un-American venom of these groups that poisoned the very atmosphere that Americans breathed. That insensitivity is the reason we could go off to war in 1941 and, with a jim crow army, fight one country that touted its Aryan supremacy and another country of darker peoples whose citizens were made honorary Aryans!

Following World War II we still had to confront the very problems at home that we scarcely recognized as having existed a decade or so earlier. In the decade following World War II, this country seriously confronted the problem of de jure and de facto racial segregation in the schools. Thus, in the middle of the twentieth century, the world's leading democracy was torn apart over whether white children and black children could go to the same schools and begin at an early age to learn something about each other and to recognize and appreciate those transcendent human qualities that have nothing to do with color.

Since we were so late in recognizing and beginning to confront the color line in education, it comes as no great surprise that problems relating to it persist. From the time that African Americans sought to have their own homes and engage in work other than domestic or personal service, they have been unwelcome neighbors to white Americans. If they sought housing in or near a white neighborhood, either they were denied the opportunity or, if they succeeded in securing housing, whites began to leave the neighborhood. They fled to all-white enclaves where the schools would be all-white or largely white.

In Durham, North Carolina, there are two high schools. One of them has not one white student and the other has only a few. Where have all the white students gone? They have either enrolled in private schools in the city or enrolled in schools out in the county to which their parents have fled. The economic ramifications of such moves are far-reaching since they take with them much of the healthy tax base that had previously been available to the city schools. And many of the commercial and industrial institutions joined in the flight, placing them beyond urban African Americans seeking employment opportunities.

In Durham at the present time there is a drive on to merge the county and city schools, led by groups who believe it will improve the quality of both systems. Although the drive has considerable support, there is real opposition. Some African Americans oppose the merger because they see it as a move to divest them of the leadership roles they now enjoy in the city schools, where the superintendent and many of the school principals are African Americans. Some white Americans oppose it because, they argue, the "inefficient operations" that characterize the city schools will contaminate the county schools. The real problem is that the county schools, even with some African American students, are the refuge of white parents and their progeny, while the city schools are essentially the schools for African American children. Thus, in 1992, we have in Durham and in many, many other communities across the nation the dual school system that was theoretically dispatched in 1954 in *Brown v. The Board of Education.*

It is so difficult in our country to establish and maintain communities that have a healthy mix of white Americans, African Americans, Asians, Latinos, and other groups that are an essential part of the American landscape. The attempt to maintain such a community is reminiscent of trying to begin a horse race, with this or that horse breaking out of the stall before the signal goes off to start the race. The difficulty in maintaining such communities arises from the problem of housing, we are told. Even after restrictive covenants were declared to be unenforceable in 1948 in *Shelley v. Kraemer,* white Americans sought by every method possible, from redlining to intimidation, to keep African Americans out of *their* community.[5] Ugly incidents continue as reminders that the color line in housing is alive and well. A kind of illness has come over people who undertake to determine for themselves who should live next door or on the block or, indeed, anywhere in the

5. 334 U.S. 605 (1948).

neighborhood. When an African American family moves in, the question never is "What church will they attend" or "How many boys and how many girls are in the family" or "Will their parents have time, with both of them working, to be active in the PTA." Before such healthy, normal questions can be raised, the whites put their houses up for sale, and thus another opportunity is lost to eliminate the color line.

If the color line persists in education and housing, it goes without saying that it exists in employment. From the beginning, Africans in the New World were relegated to the role of hewers of wood and drawers of water. Consequently, they made ideal slaves, sufficiently obsequious to take orders from their superiors and *never* insubordinate or independent. At least this is what the owners claimed, although current research tells us otherwise. In any case, there was sufficient commitment on the part of the dominant group to keep slaves under control, and to force blacks who were free to steer clear of occupations where they might compete with white workers. Thus, it was possible to prevent a free person in a free country from pursuing his occupation or trade simply because the city or the state did not want him to compete with a white person for employment. This was the beginning of preferential treatment or affirmative action in the workplace, this time in behalf of whites.

In the nineteenth and twentieth centuries, there was always strong resistance to African Americans moving into new occupations or industries. They were regarded as out of place except in menial roles or personal service. When the textile industry came to the southern states in the 1880s, African Americans were barred from all except custodial tasks in the mills. There were no black operatives in spinning and weaving. Employment in those areas was reserved for white men and women, many of whom came out of the small hamlets and mountains to perform these privileged tasks. The best job open to an African American man was to sweep the floors and keep the place clean, while an African American woman was fortunate if she secured a job as maid in one of the company-owned homes of a husband and wife, both of whom had found employment in the mill. Earlier it would have been unthinkable for these mountain folk to have had servants. Now it was possible, thanks to the exclusion of blacks from the factory workplace.

Meanwhile, the strong resistance to African Americans moving into new occupations or new industries continued. The fear was ever-present that they might be securing jobs that would otherwise be available to some prospective white workers. And this fear was informed by a strong belief that the African American was not qualified to hold the job anyway. The watchword of the white worker was that the best way to keep the black man down was to keep him out of a job. And if the white worker was opposed to his employment, the white employer could use him only to help break a strike. In recent years, the strength of labor unions was seriously undermined by the encouragement that the public and the government gave to employers to break strikes by hiring permanent white replacements.

Indeed, the government has taken an active role in placing beyond the reach of laborers, especially African Americans, the protections that legislation has offered.

In 1972 Congress amended the Civil Rights Act in order to give the courts the authority to require affirmative action measures to compensate for discriminatory practices. Unless some numerical goals were established or specific measures taken to bring about the hiring of additional African Americans, it was unlikely that public or private employers would take the initiative in correcting past discriminatory practices. The conservative majority on the United States Supreme Court, moreover, took the position that the Civil Rights Act provided relief only for those aggrieved employees or prospective employees who could prove that they were not hired or not promoted because of racial discrimination.[6] And the court insisted that "set aside" programs, by which a certain portion of public contracts would be awarded to minority contractors, violated the rights of those competing contractors who happened to be white.[7]

The court held in 1971 that employment practices which disproportionately exclude minorities and women are unlawful unless employers can show that such practices are a business necessity, and that any employment practice "which cannot be shown to be related to job performance . . . is prohibited."[8] In 1989 the court, now safely conservative, thanks to appointments by President Reagan, could insist that the Civil Rights Act of 1866 did not protect an employee's rights *after* the contract had been established, including breach of the terms of the contract or the imposition of discrimina-

6. *Wards Cove Packing Company, Inc. v. Atonio,* 57 U.S.L.W. 4583.
7. *City of Richmond v. J. A. Crosson Co.,* 488 U.S. 469 (1988).
8. *Griggs v. Duke Power Co.,* 401 U.S. 424 (1971).

tory working conditions.[9] It was this decision and rulings in similar cases that caused the Congress to consider new civil rights legislation to correct the course the Supreme Court had taken.

For President Bush and his conservative free-market colleagues, affirmative action programs and "set aside" arrangements were merely "quota" requirements that had no place in a free society. When, therefore, Congress undertook to clarify its position and its support of affirmative action, the president accused it of establishing "quotas," which he regarded as unconstitutional. He stood his ground through the 1990 elections against the efforts of Congress to countermand decisions by the Supreme Court. His veto of the civil rights bill in 1990 was the first time a president had vetoed such a bill since Andrew Johnson turned back the civil rights bill of 1866. Johnson was overridden; but Bush was not. Bush retreated the following year, however, when the groundswell of public opinion and his own party leaders in Congress forced him to make the specious claim that the new legislation passed by the Congress was not a "quotas" bill as was the one he had vetoed in 1990, and he could therefore sign it.

Although administration spokesmen such as C. Boyden Gray, the president's counsel on domestic issues, attempted to make the case that the bill's sponsors had compromised and eliminated the so-called "quotas" aspect of the bill, they were not successful in doing so. It was clear to anyone who cared to look that the president had reached the point where it was no longer politically profitable to fight the new civil rights bill. As Professor Paul Gewirtz of the Yale Law School stated,

9. *Patterson v. McLean Credit Union*, 485 U.S. 617 (1989).

the final agreement on the civil rights bill "won virtually everything that civil rights advocates sought two years ago."[10]

It was one thing for the president to be involved in questionable employment practices in the private sector. It was quite another thing for the executive branch of the government to be thrown on the defensive because of its own questionable employment practices. Many areas of public service have been accused of employment discrimination as far as African Americans are concerned. Indeed, the several features of existing civil rights bills do not apply to the day-to-day operations, hiring practices, or personnel policies of the Congress, the White House, or the Supreme Court.

There are, however, affirmative action officers in the several departments and agencies. But the overgrown bureaucracy is generally impervious to such problems as employment practices, racial quotas, and the like. Seldom is the situation desperate enough to become a part of public discussion. Despite its mysterious and undercover operations, the Federal Bureau of Investigation has in recent years become the target of open criticism by its African American agents and other minority employees.

African Americans had been wary of the FBI for many years. Some of them knew of its voluminous files on the National Association for the Advancement of Colored People, and even the National Urban League, that dated as far back as the 1920s. Many knew of J. Edgar Hoover's

10. Quoted in William T. Coleman, Jr., and Vernon E. Jordan, Jr., "How the Civil Rights Bill Was Really Passed," *Washington Post,* November 18, 1991. This article was specifically written to refute C. Boyden Gray's claim that the advocates of the civil rights bill had made important concessions, and that was why President Bush could sign the bill.

deep antipathy to Martin Luther King, Jr., and the objectives for which he fought. Almost nothing was known of FBI employment practices or racial policies until a few years ago, when one African American agent charged his colleagues with racial harassment, including death threats, and the bureau with racial discrimination in promotions and assignments. After seven years of litigation the case was quietly settled in the complainant's favor.[11]

Then, in April 1991, approximately three hundred African American FBI agents presented a list of grievances to the director, William S. Sessions. They threatened a class-action suit against the bureau, charging it with discrimination in promotions, transfers, and assignments. This legacy of unfairness against minorities dated back to the reign of J. Edgar Hoover.

During the year following their charges, the representatives of the African American FBI agents met regularly with the director of the bureau or his representatives, and by April 1992 the two sides had reached substantial agreement in a number of important areas that reflected several significant concessions on the part of the bureau. It would immediately promote six black agents to supervisory jobs and place thirteen others in the management training program. It agreed to reassign fifteen black agents to its more desirable smaller field offices "where responsibility is often greater" and to "open fifteen more training slots for black agents." The FBI also agreed to open up new opportunities for African Americans in areas and departments where they were underrepresented. It also agreed to give some of the black

11. *New York Times*, August 9, 1990, A24, and August 10, 1990, A13.

agents back pay and other payments to make up for the disparities "in how it awards bonuses in proportions similar to those given to white agents."

The FBI refused to admit that it had discriminated against African American agents or that discrimination had occurred.[12] One suspects that this is standard, perhaps universal policy. A few months ago when a motorist did several thousand dollars worth of damage to my car, his insurance company undertook to pay for all repairs, for the depreciation in value to my car that the accident had caused, and for five weeks rental of a new automobile *IF* I permitted the company to declare that neither it nor its insured client admitted any responsibility for the accident. That presented no insurmountable obstacle for me any more than a similar caveat presented an obstacle for the black FBI agents.

There was an undercurrent of resentment among some white agents when they learned of the bureau's agreement with black agents. They complained that the bureau was giving minorities unfair promotion advantages. Apparently they had nothing to say about the decades during which the bureau held back African American agents to the very great advantage of white agents. But that is the way it has always been, and it is predictable. Whenever an effort is made to redress a wrong done to a certain group, some members of the group that has never experienced a wrong tend to feel aggrieved. They are displeased simply because justice has at long last been done to the group whose disadvantaged position provided new opportunities for those who now protest what they call reverse discrimination.

More than two in five black children live in poverty in

12. *New York Times*, April 22, 1992.

this, the richest country in the world. Head Start programs, which have proved to be spectacularly successful, serve only a fifth of eligible low-income children because we cannot afford to finance the program for all eligible children. Life expectancy among African Americans has dropped at a time when some of the greatest advances in medical science have been made. Even on Medicare, older African American patients get heart bypass operations only about a fourth as often as their white counterparts. The rate of unemployment among African Americans is generally twice that among white Americans. Disparities such as these exist in virtually every area of life touching on African Americans and white Americans. Worse still, they inform the attitudes of racial groups toward each other more than they inform public policy, which is supposed to deal with the problems these disparities reveal.

The color line is alive, well, and flourishing in the final decade of the twentieth century. It thrives because we have been desensitized to its significance over two centuries, and it permeates our thinking and our actions on matters as far apart figuratively as New York's Harlem and New York's Upper East Side, or an African American mayor of Los Angeles and the videotaped beating of Rodney King by four members of the Los Angeles Police Department. There is nothing inherently wrong with being aware of color as long as it is seen as making distinctions in a pleasant, superficial, and unimportant manner. It is only when character is attached to color, when ability is measured by color, when privilege is tied to color, and a whole galaxy of factors that spell the difference between success and failure in our society are tied to color—it is only when such considerations are attached to color that it becomes a deadly, dreadful, denigrating factor among us all. It is when it is such a factor that we have two nations, black and white, separate, hostile, unequal.

It seems pointless to argue that African Americans should cease seeing themselves as victims of a heartless social and economic order that owes them much more than they have ever received. It would appear to be equally pointless for others to claim that enough has already been done for African Americans and that from this point forward they must fend for themselves. African Americans are, indeed, the victims of centuries of exploitation and injustice, but acknowledging that fact alone will not forge a policy for the future. Likewise, African Americans need to help themselves perhaps even more than they have done up to this point, although it seems obvious that if they had the proper tools of education, better health care, housing, and equal treatment under the law, they could do much better. It does no good to pull out all the code words and phrases, as President Bush and others have done, and decry "deadbeats" and "cycle of dependency," for that plays into the hands of those who respond to racial politics. The cycle of dependency and the deadbeats are not all on one side. Government subsidies for business, government bailouts for failing savings and loan associations and banks, government reduction or elimination of capital gains taxes, and government support of oil depletion allowances also help to create a cycle of dependency.

We now live in an age when the role of government is inevitably important whether we are referring to preschool education in Seattle or the aircraft industry in that area, whether we are talking about welfare in Detroit or the creaky, wavering automotive industry there. What we need so desperately is the assumption of responsibility at the highest levels in the public *and* private sectors to make a strong pitch for the elimination of the uglier aspects of the color line so that we can have a healthier, happier, even gentler society. We need to appreciate the importance of legislation, judicial decisions, and executive orders in setting the stage for eliminating the color line. Without them it is not possible for individuals or groups of individuals, however dedicated, to make a good-faith and successful effort to eliminate the color line. Yet we cannot expect too much of these public efforts, important as they are. These public efforts must be combined with private efforts to promote mutual respect and a willingness to make judgments of others based on what they have done and can do, and not on who they are. If we can somehow teach ourselves these lessons in human relations, perhaps we can take the first feeble steps toward creating the kind of community about which some of our forebears spoke and wrote, and the kind of nation about which so many of us have dreamed but never realized.

Perhaps the very first thing we need to do as a nation and as individual members of society is to confront our past and see it for what it is. It is a past that is filled with some of the ugliest possible examples of racial brutality and degradation in human history. We need to recognize it for what it was and is and not explain it away, excuse it, or justify it. Having done that, we should then make a good-faith effort to turn our history around so that we can see it in front of us, so that we can avoid doing what we have done for so long. If we do that, whites will discover that African Americans possess the same human qualities that other Americans possess, and African Americans will discover that white Americans are capable of the most sublime expressions of human conduct of which all human beings are capable. Then, we need to do everything possible to emphasize the positive qualities that all of us have, qualities which we have never utilized to the fullest, but which we must utilize if we are to solve the problem of the color line in the twenty-first century.

INDEX

ABOUT THE AUTHOR

John Hope Franklin is the James B. Duke Professor Emeritus of History and from 1985 to 1992 was Professor of Legal History in the Law School at Duke University. A native of Oklahoma, he received a B.A. degree from Fisk University and A.M. and Ph.D. degrees in history from Harvard University. He has taught at a number of institutions, including Fisk University, North Carolina Central University, Howard University, and Brooklyn College. In 1964 he joined the faculty of the University of Chicago, serving as Chairman of the Department of History from 1967 to 1970. He was the John Matthews Manly Distinguished Service Professor from 1969 to 1982, when he became Emeritus Professor there.

Professor Franklin's books include *From Slavery to Freedom: A History of Negro Americans*, *The Emancipation Proclamation*, *The Militant South*, *The Free Negro in North Carolina*, *Reconstruction After the Civil War*, and *A Southern Odyssey: Travelers in the Antebellum North*. His Jefferson Lecture in the Humanities for 1976 was published under the title *Racial Equality in America*. His *George Washington Williams: A Biography*, which was published in 1985, received the Clarence L. Holte Literary Prize for that year. A selection of essays covering a teaching and writing career of fifty years was published in 1990 under the title *Race and History: Selected Essays, 1938–1988* and received the Hayden University Prize. His current research deals with "Dissidents on the Plantation: Runaway Slaves."

Through the years he has been active in professional and educational organizations. For many years he served on the editorial board of the *Journal of Negro History*, and he has served as president of the American Studies Association (1967), the Southern Historical Association (1970), the United Chapters of Phi Beta Kappa (1973–1976), the Organization of American Historians (1975), and the American Historical Association (1979).

Professor Franklin has served on many national commissions and delegations, including the National Council on the Humanities, from which he resigned in 1979, when the president appointed him to the Advisory Commission on Public Diplomacy. Another appointment was membership of the President's Advisory Commission on Ambassadorial Appointments. In September and October 1980, he was a United States delegate to the 21st General Conference of UNESCO. Among his many other foreign assignments he has served as Pitt Professor of American History and Institutions of Cambridge University, Consultant on American Education in the Soviet Union, Fulbright Professor in Australia, and Lecturer in American History in the People's Republic of China. In recent years he has been a member of the Board of Trustees of Fisk University, the Chicago Public Library, and the Chicago Symphony Orchestra Association.

He has been the recipient of many honors, among them the Jefferson Medal for 1984, awarded by the Council for the Advancement and Support of Education, the Cleanth Brooks Medal awarded by the Fellowship of Southern Writers in 1989, and in 1990 the Encyclopedia

Britannica Gold Medal for the Dissemination of Knowledge. In 1978 he was elected to the Oklahoma Hall of Fame, and in the same year was one of eight Americans cited by *Who's Who in America* for significant contributions to society. He has received honorary degrees from more than ninety colleges and universities.